Earth & Space Science

MW01182119

Giant Hurricanes and Tornadoes

by
Alan Venable

Don Johnston Incorporated
Volo, Illinois

Edited by:

John Bergez
Start-to-Finish Core Content Series Editor, Pacifica, California

Barbara Armentrout, MA
Start-to-Finish Core Content Developmental Editor, San Carlos, California

Gail Portnuff Venable, MS, CCC-SLP
Speech/Language Pathologist, San Francisco, California

Dorothy Tyack, MA
Learning Disabilities Specialist, San Francisco, California

Jerry Stemach, MS, CCC-SLP
Speech/Language Pathologist, Director of Content Development, Sonoma County, California

Expert review:

Jorge Vazquez, Ph.D
Project Scientist Physical Oceanography Distributed Active Archive Center (PO.DAAC), JPL/NASA/Caltech

Graphics and Illustrations:

Photographs and illustrations are all created professionally and modified to provide the best possible support for the intended reader.
Front cover: © Eric Nguyen/Jim Reed Photography/Corbis
Pages 9, 12, 16, 27, 30-32, 52-53, 55-56, and back cover: Courtesy of the NOAA
Page 15: Courtesy of the U.S. Air Force, photo by Staff Sgt. Randy Redman
Page 17: © Scott Smith
Page 19: © 2005, courtesy of the NOAA National Severe Storms Lab
Page 29: Courtesy of FEMA/Mark Wolfe
Page 38: Courtesy of FEMA News, Photo by Anita Westervelt
Page 42: Courtesy of the U.S. Navy, photo by Photographer's Mate Airman Richard R. Waite
Page 45: Courtesy of Brian E. Smith, National Weather Service
Page 51: © Andrew Fox/Corbis
All other photos not credited here or with the photo are © Don Johnston Incorporated and its licensors.

Narration:

Professional actors and actresses read the text to build excitement and to model research-based elements of fluency: intonation, stress, prosody, phrase groupings and rate. The rate has been set to maximize comprehension for the reader.

Published by:

Don Johnston Incorporated
26799 West Commerce Drive
Volo, IL 60073

800.999.4660 USA Canada
800.889.5242 Technical Support
www.donjohnston.com

International Standard Book Number
ISBN: 978-1-4105-0873-7

Contents

Produced in cooperation with the NASA/Caltech-Jet Propulsion Laboratory Education Office,
Project Scientist Physical Oceanography Distributed Active Archive Center (PO.DAAC)

DON JOHNSTON

Getting Started

Tornado! thought Will Keller. He had seen the tall tower of wind spinning across the fields. Keller knew that the tall funnel shape meant big trouble. He yelled to his wife and kids to get down into the tornado cellar as fast as they could. The tornado cellar was an underground shelter that Keller had built. It was just a few yards from the house.

The family ran for the cellar. Keller planned to follow them and pull the door shut behind him. But he stopped to watch as the **tornado** came closer. He saw that there were *three* tornadoes — not just one. The two smaller tornadoes were twisting around in the sky like giant ropes.

Will Keller risked his life to watch a tornado in Kansas in 1928.

The big tornado hung down right in the center of a huge storm cloud. The tornado had already torn a wide path through Keller's fields, and now the mouth of the tornado (the bottom end) began to lift up off the ground.

That mouth will pass right over us! Keller thought. *I have to watch!*

Keller held on to the cellar door as the storm came closer. In a few seconds, the shaggy end of the funnel hung right over his head. Suddenly, everything was as still as death. Keller could hardly breathe. Then a screaming hiss came from the end of the funnel. Keller was looking straight up into the tornado.

What did Keller see up there? You will find out later in this book.

This book is about the power of tornadoes. It is also about **hurricanes**. Both tornadoes and hurricanes are circles of wind that spin very fast.

A tornado is a spinning tower of very fast wind that moves along the ground. Tornadoes usually happen during thunderstorms.

A hurricane is a giant rainstorm with clouds that spin in a circle. Hurricanes start as thunderstorms over the ocean.

How much damage can these winds do? How do scientists get close enough to study them? What other stories do people tell about tornadoes and hurricanes? Are these stories true? You will find the answers to these questions in this book.

Article 1

Studying Monster Storms

Questions this article will answer:

• **How do scientists study hurricanes?**

• **How do scientists study tornadoes?**

"OK, everyone! Check your seatbelts. It's time to rock and roll!"

The words of the pilot sound like he's having fun, but his hands are sweating on the controls of his airplane. The plane is made for studying the weather, and the pilot is about to fly it into the center of a hurricane.

As the plane flies into the milky white clouds, drops of water shoot over the windows. Strong winds toss the plane around and shake the scientists in their seats.

This is what you would see from a plane in the center of a hurricane.

The pilot's voice comes over the intercom. He wants to keep everyone in a good mood, so he asks them a riddle. "OK, guys," he says. "Guess which way we're flying."

"North?" one of the scientists asks.

"Northeast?" asks another.

"Wrong," the pilot answers. "There's no way to tell which way we're flying. All I know for sure is that we are flying *sideways*!"

When a weather plane flies into the **eye wall** of a hurricane, the plane can be tossed in many directions. The eye wall is a circle of thunderstorms spinning around the **eye** (center) of a hurricane. If the pilot isn't lucky, the slamming winds can rip off a wing. After all, those winds may hit the airplane sideways at up to 200 miles (320 kilometers) per hour.

It's important for scientists to study hurricanes and tornadoes because these storms cause huge amounts of damage. But hurricanes and tornadoes are not easy to study. It's dangerous work, of course, but there are other problems, too. This article tells how scientists study the secrets of hurricanes and tornadoes.

Studying Hurricanes

Scientists study hurricanes for two reasons. First, they want to learn what causes hurricanes. Second, they want information to help them guess what a hurricane is going to do next. This is called **forecasting**. Scientists need to be able to forecast how fast the wind will be and where the hurricane will go. Then they are able to warn people who live in the path of the storm.

To study a hurricane, scientists need to get close to it and gather huge amounts of **data** (information). They must gather the data quickly, and they must study it quickly, using computers. The job is hard, and it can be dangerous.

Scientists study lots of data to understand what hurricanes do.

Here is some of the information that scientists collect from the hurricane:

- The speed and direction of the wind

- The temperature of the air inside and outside the hurricane

- The temperature of the ocean below the hurricane

- The amount of water that's in the air inside the hurricane

It isn't easy for scientists to collect all this data, but they have some special tools to help them. Weather airplanes use two special inventions to gather data about hurricanes. One invention collects data from inside hurricanes. The other invention collects data about hurricanes even when they are far away.

The first invention that collects data from inside a hurricane is called a **sonde**. A sonde is a special kind of tube that holds tools for measuring weather. The sonde is dropped from a plane into the hurricane. As the sonde falls through the hurricane's clouds, it measures the temperature of the air at many levels. It also measures the speed of the wind. Then, when the sonde drops into the sea, it measures the temperature of the water at different levels below the surface. The sonde uses radio signals to send all the data back up to the plane.

This sonde will be dropped from
an airplane into a hurricane.

The second invention is **Doppler radar**.
A Doppler radar machine on a weather plane
sends out radio waves that can measure
hurricanes when they are still far away.

When the Doppler waves hit something, they bounce back to the radar machine. A computer measures the signals as they come back. These signals tell scientists how far away the object is. Doppler radar can tell how fast a hurricane is moving. It can also tell which direction the hurricane is going. It can even tell how much water is in hurricane clouds many miles away.

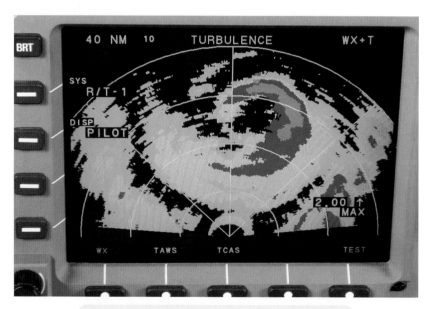

Doppler radar machines show the size and shape of hurricanes.

Chasing Tornadoes

Tornadoes are much smaller than hurricanes, but are they easier to study? The answer is "No!" Some of the same kinds of inventions are used, but tornadoes are harder to study.

Tornadoes are hard to study up close!

To study a tornado, scientists have to collect a lot of data on temperature, wind, and moisture (water) in the air. But most tornadoes only last for a few seconds or minutes, so it's hard to get the data fast enough. And even when a tornado lasts an hour or more, it's hard for scientists to keep track of it. This is because the tornado can change its shape and its direction as it moves. And these changes may also be hidden by clouds and sheets of rain.

Storm chasers are scientists who travel around looking for big storms to study. They hope to watch tornadoes as they happen and to collect data about them. Storm chasers may spend months and months driving around, trying to find a good tornado to study.

Storm chasers use special inventions like the ones that hurricane scientists use. Some storm chasers drive trucks that carry Doppler radar machines. Other chasers drive trucks that carry **probes**. A tornado probe holds tools for collecting data about tornadoes. The tools are protected by a heavy metal shell.

This Doppler radar truck is used to collect data about tornadoes.

Storm "chasing" is really more like sneaking up on a tornado. Storm chasers try to leave their probes on the ground right in the path of a tornado. Then the chasers have to get away fast!

This storm chaser is trying to put a probe in the tornado's path.

After the tornado has passed, they come back and look for the probes. If they are lucky, the tornado has passed close to the probes so that the probes could pick up data. And if they are *really* lucky, the tornado has not smashed the probes!

Summary

In this article, you learned why hurricanes and tornadoes are hard to study. Danger is just one of the problems. Another problem is that scientists have to collect huge amounts of data in very little time.

Weather scientists use special tools to study hurricanes and tornadoes. Scientists studying hurricanes use Doppler radar and sondes. Scientists studying tornadoes use Doppler radar and probes.

Storm chasers place probes on the ground in the path of a tornado. Scientists use computers to make sense of all their data.

Article 2

The Power of Hurricanes

Questions this article will answer:

• **How big and how strong are hurricanes?**

• **How do hurricanes do their damage?**

Hurricanes are called different things in different parts of the world. Scientists often use the name **tropical cyclone** when they talk about hurricanes. A tropical cyclone is a spinning storm that is born over an ocean. If a storm begins over the Atlantic Ocean, it is called a *hurricane*.

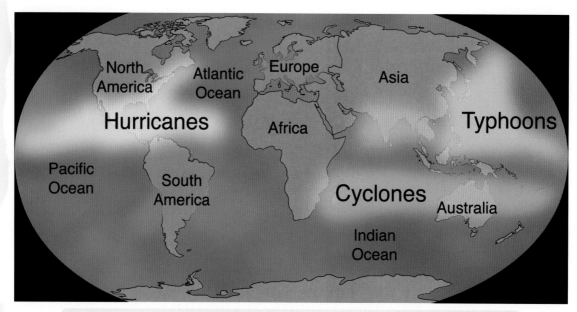

North America · Atlantic Ocean · Europe · Asia

Hurricanes · Africa · **Typhoons**

Pacific Ocean · South America · **Cyclones** · Australia

Indian Ocean

Hurricanes are called different things in different parts of the world.

If a storm begins over the Pacific Ocean and heads toward Japan or China, it is called a typhoon. But in Australia and in the countries around the Indian Ocean, these storms are called *tropical cyclones* or just *cyclones*.

Today, hurricanes that come from the Atlantic Ocean get names like Alice, Bob, or Carlos, which sound nice and friendly.

But these storms are not friends —
they're killers. Here's a list of some big
tropical cyclones and the numbers of people
they killed.

1900

Galveston, Texas   6000 dead

1970

Bangladesh, Indian Ocean   1 million dead

1974

Honduras, Central America

(Hurricane Fifi)   9000 dead

1991

Bangladesh, Indian Ocean   100,000 dead

1998

Honduras, Central America

(Hurricane Mitch)   9000 dead

How powerful are hurricanes? And how do they cause damage? You'll find out in this article.

The Power and Size of Hurricanes

A hurricane is a huge, warm, spinning storm with very fast winds. A hurricane can last for many days, and it can travel a long way. It can also dump huge amounts of rain.

A hurricane starts as a small storm over the ocean. If the water in the ocean is warm enough, the small storm gets bigger and stronger. A storm becomes known as a hurricane when its winds reach 74 miles (120 kilometers) per hour. The winds of a giant hurricane can be faster than 200 miles (320 kilometers) per hour. A hurricane can grow to be about 300 miles (480 kilometers) wide. A really big one might be 700 miles (1125 kilometers) wide.

In August 2005, Hurricane Katrina came roaring across the Atlantic Ocean and struck the southern coast of the United States. Katrina was about 460 miles (740 kilometers) wide, and its winds reached 215 miles (344 kilometers) per hour. Katrina was a giant hurricane.

This photo was taken from space. It shows Hurricane Katrina heading for the coasts of Louisiana, Mississippi, and Alabama.

27

Scientists have a list of names that they give to hurricanes. When they get to the end of the list of names, they go back to the beginning and use the same names again. But some hurricanes cause so much damage that their names are taken off the list. Hurricane Katrina flooded the city of New Orleans in Louisiana. Katrina also wrecked many other places in Louisiana, Mississippi, and Alabama. Parents may still name their babies Katrina, but no new hurricane will ever have that name.

This is all that was left of one middle school
in Mississippi after Hurricane Katrina.

How Hurricanes Do Their Damage

There are three ways that hurricanes can
cause damage. The first is wind, the second
is rain, and the third is a storm surge (a giant
wave from the ocean). This section tells
about these three kinds of problems.

The first main cause of damage is very
high winds.

In 1999, Hurricane Floyd smashed into the east coast of the United States. It hit the coast of North Carolina at 110 miles (about 175 kilometers) per hour. At that speed, wind can knock down buildings and send their roofs sailing into the sky.

The wind from Hurricane Andrew pounded this board through the palm tree.

The second main cause of damage is very heavy rain. Hurricanes can deliver tons of rain. Hurricane Floyd dumped 19 inches of rain on the town of Wilmington, North Carolina.

30

The city was flooded. In some places, there were snakes swimming in the high water that filled the streets. And many of these snakes were poisonous!

In 1998, Hurricane Mitch dumped huge amounts of rain on Honduras, a country in Central America. The rain caused such bad floods and mudslides that most of the country was destroyed.

The rains from Hurricane Mitch caused huge mudslides in Honduras.

The third main cause of damage is the storm surge. A storm surge is a giant wave that is pushed along by a hurricane. The wave can be 30 feet (10 meters) high when it hits land. Hurricane Floyd's storm surge was about 11 feet (3.5 meters) high. In 1900, Galveston, Texas was hit by a surge that was about 16 feet (5 meters) high. The surge killed at least 6000 people.

This storm surge struck the coast of Florida during a hurricane in 1975. This wave was 16 feet (almost 5 meters) high.

When the storm surge hit Galveston, there were no good warning systems. In those days, storm surges caused most of the deaths from hurricanes in the United States. But today, scientists have tools to see hurricanes when the storms are still far from land. So now scientists can warn people to get out of the way of a storm surge. This kind of warning saves many lives.

Some parts of the world still do not have good warning systems. At the beginning of this article, you read that tropical cyclones killed one million people in Bangladesh in 1970 and 100,000 people in 1991. Storm surges caused most of those deaths. In Bangladesh, millions of people live on islands and lowlands near the sea, so even when the people are warned, most of them cannot get away quickly.

Summary

In this article, you learned that a hurricane or other tropical cyclone can kill many thousands of people. These storms bring mighty winds and huge amounts of rain.

Hurricanes cause damage with their heavy winds, heavy rains, and storm surges. In some parts of the world, it is still impossible to warn everyone to get out of the way before the storm surge comes.

Article 3

The Twisted Truth About Tornadoes

Questions this article will answer:

- Do tornadoes hit schools and trailer parks more often than other places?

- Can tornadoes make fish rain down from the sky?

- Can tornadoes lift cars and cows into the air?

In the movie called *Twister*, a tornado seems to lift a truck straight up in the air. In the movie *The Wizard of Oz*, a farmer milks a cow that is floating up into the clouds. Of course, the farmer milking the floating cow is a joke. But can tornadoes really do the other things that we have seen in Hollywood movies?

A tornado has amazing power. It is a spinning tower of very fast wind that moves along the ground. The speed of a tornado's wind is at least 40 miles (64 kilometers) per hour, and it can go as fast as 300 miles (480 kilometers) per hour. And tornadoes often appear with big storms that have rain, lightning, and hail.

But are any of the wild stories true, or are they all myths (made-up stories that have been told for a long time)? This article describes three wild ideas about tornadoes.

One idea is that tornadoes hit mobile homes and schools more than other places. The second idea is that tornadoes can make the sky rain fish. And the third idea is that tornadoes can lift cows and other heavy things high into the sky.

Are these ideas true, or are they myths? What do you think?

Targets of Tornadoes

Most of the people who are killed by tornadoes are in cars or mobile homes. That much is true for sure.

This mobile home was hit by a weak tornado.

Some people believe that tornadoes hit schools and trailer parks more than anything else. They think that trailer parks attract tornadoes because the trailers are lined up in rows. And they think that the streets between the rows give a tornado a path to follow.

But these ideas are myths.

It is true that small swirls of wind called *dust devils* often blow through the streets of trailer parks. But a dust devil is not a tornado.

Schools and mobile homes do not really *attract* tornadoes. It's just that we pay more attention when places like these are destroyed. A TV station might not think it's big news if a small tornado pulls some trees out of the ground or knocks down one barn. But if that same tornado knocks down the walls of a school or wipes out half a trailer park, that *is* big news.

Even a small tornado can destroy mobile homes because their walls are thin, and they may not be attached strongly to the ground.

If a mobile home is not well attached to the ground, it can be destroyed by a weak tornado that is blowing only 60 to 70 miles per hour (97 to 113 kilometers per hour).

Fish from the Sky

Do you believe that fish can rain down from the sky? A man named John Lewis said that this happened to him one day in February 1859 in the United Kingdom.

Lewis said, "Suddenly little fish were falling all over me, down my neck, and on my head. I took off my hat, and the brim was full of them! All around me, the ground was suddenly covered with jumping fish . . . . We filled a bucket with some of the fish and took them to the London Zoo, and those fish were still alive!"

Can fish really fall out of the sky?

Lewis's wild story was true. Many people saw it happen and wrote down what they saw. For thousands of years, there have been stories of fish, frogs, snails, and other animals falling from the sky. Some of those stories have been true, too.

Probably these things happen because a tornado or a waterspout passes over an ocean or a lake and sucks up some small fish or other animals. A **waterspout** is a kind of tornado that travels over water instead of land. Tornadoes and waterspouts can lift small animals into winds that will carry them for many miles. The fish or frogs may land in a place where people never even saw the tornado or the storm that made it.

A waterspout is a tornado that happens over water.

Lifting Cows

Next, let's look at the stories of cows and cars flying by in tornadoes. Can these stories be true?

Can tornadoes really make cows fly?

Tornadoes have two kinds of wind blowing at the same time. One kind of wind blows sideways. We call this a **horizontal** wind. The other kind of wind blows upward. We call this a **vertical** wind. The twisting horizontal wind can blow at a speed of 300 miles (480 kilometers) per hour. The lifting vertical wind does not blow as fast. It can blow at a speed of 100 miles (160 kilometers) per hour. Is that vertical wind strong enough to lift a truck or a cow straight up into the air?

The answer is "No." An upward wind of 100 miles per hour is *not* strong enough to lift a cow straight up. But the important words are *straight up*. A tornado does not need to lift a cow straight up in order to carry it away.

The vertical wind can lift the cow slightly off the ground, and then the stronger horizontal wind carries it sideways. Tornadoes can throw cars and trucks sideways, too. And a tornado can move a heavy roof in the same way. It lifts the roof and blows it sideways at the same time. The roof "takes off" and sails up into the air.

A strong tornado picked up this school bus and flipped it over.

Heavy objects usually spin out of a tornado before they go up more than 200 feet (60 meters). But the strongest tornadoes can carry a car for half a mile (almost a kilometer). They can also carry people. In May 1930, a tornado struck the home of Lawrence Kern in Kickapoo, Kansas. It carried Kern more than a mile. He was still alive when he landed, but his head was buried in the ground and he soon died.

Light objects can be carried several miles. In 1925, a tornado in the United States carried a pair of pants high into the sky. There, they caught a stream of wind and traveled 39 miles (63 kilometers). When they came down, there was still $95 in one of the pockets!

Summary

In this article, you learned that some amazing stories about tornadoes are true. Other tornado stories are myths. It is a myth that schools and trailer parks attract tornadoes. It is also a myth that tornadoes can lift cows and other heavy things straight up into the sky. But it is true that a waterspout or a tornado can cause fish or small animals to rain down from the sky.

Article 4

Tornado Alley

Questions this article will answer:

• **What is Tornado Alley?**

• **What are tornado swarms and outbreaks?**

At the beginning of this book, you read about Will Keller, the man who looked straight up into the mouth of a tornado. Keller lived to tell the tale, and what he saw was amazing. Around the inside edges of the big tornado, small tornadoes were always forming and breaking away.

The small tornadoes looked like the tails of giant rats. Keller thought that these tails were making the hissing noise that he heard inside the tornado. Keller saw that tornado in Kansas.

Kansas is one of the states in the part of the United States called Tornado Alley. In this article you will learn more about Tornado Alley and how it got its name.

The Tornado Alley in the Middle of the United States

Tornado Alley is the name of the world's most famous tornado zone. A tornado zone is a place where many tornadoes strike. On the map on the next page, the yellow part is Tornado Alley. It covers much of the large flat part of the United States that is called the Great Plains. States next to Tornado Alley get a lot of tornadoes, too.

49

The yellow part of the United States shows Tornado Alley.

The United States holds the world record for the most tornadoes per year. It gets 800 to 1000 tornadoes a year. The United Kingdom also gets a lot of tornadoes, but they are usually smaller than the ones in Tornado Alley.

These cars were in the path of a
tornado in the United Kingdom.

Why are there so many big tornadoes
in Tornado Alley? Most tornadoes are created
by thunderstorms, and Tornado Alley is a huge
flat land where thunderstorms can build up
great power. The storms grow when a lot
of cold air and warm air run into each other.

51

A tornado in Tornado Alley

In Tornado Alley, cold air flows from the Rocky Mountains and from Canada. The cold air meets up with warm, wet air that is heading north from the Gulf of Mexico. This meeting creates many very large thunderstorms. And many of these storms create tornadoes.

Outbreaks and Swarms
in Tornado Alley

Remember what Will Keller saw before he looked straight up into the big tornado? He saw two smaller tornadoes that twisted around like ropes. What Keller saw is called a swarm of tornadoes. A **tornado swarm** is a group of tornadoes that all come from the same storm.

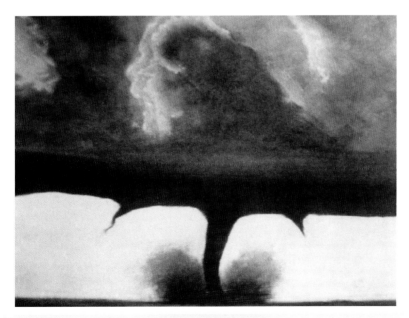

In this photo, three tornadoes are coming from the same storm.

53

Tornado Alley is famous for tornado swarms and tornado outbreaks. In a **tornado outbreak**, ten or more tornadoes happen in the same area within a few days. Tornado outbreaks can be bad around Tornado Alley. Here are a couple of examples.

During two days in May 1999, a huge tornado outbreak ripped through Oklahoma and Kansas. The storms killed 43 people and destroyed thousands of houses. About 45 tornadoes hit Oklahoma, and 14 hit Kansas. At least one tornado was a mile (1.6 kilometers) wide. Winds in some of the tornadoes were faster than 207 miles (333 kilometers) per hour. In Oklahoma City, whole neighborhoods were blown apart.

A tornado in an outbreak in Oklahoma did this.

During one week in May 2003, 393 tornadoes were reported over 19 states. This was the worst week of **severe weather** (very bad weather) in the history of the United States. The tornado winds caused many deaths and heavy damage, and hail from the same storms caused damage, too.

55

Think about getting hit by this hailstone.

Summary

In this article, you learned that Tornado Alley in the United States is the world's most famous tornado zone. There, giant thunderstorms send down many huge and deadly tornadoes every year. In Tornado Alley, tornado swarms and outbreaks kill dozens of people and cause huge amounts of damage.

In this book you learned why hurricanes and tornadoes are hard to study. You found out about some tools that scientists use to study them. You read some myths and some amazing true stories about tornadoes. You learned about the awesome power of both kinds of storms and the damage that they can do.

If you ever come close to one of these monsters, stay as safe as you can!

Glossary

Word	Definition	Page
data	information	12
Doppler radar	a tool or machine that uses radio waves to get information about objects that are far away	15
eye	the center of a **hurricane**	10
eye wall	a circle of thunderclouds around the **eye** of a **hurricane**	10
forecast	to say what the weather is going to do next	11
horizontal	side to side	44
hurricane	a giant storm with spinning winds *Hurricane* is the name for **tropical cyclones** that are born over the Atlantic Ocean.	6
probe	a tool that is put on the ground in the path of a tornado to collect information about the **tornado**	19
severe weather	very bad weather, such as thunderstorms, **tornadoes**, and **hurricanes**	55

Word	Definition	Page
sonde	a metal tube that contains tools for measuring weather A sonde is dropped into a hurricane from a weather plane.	14
storm chaser	a weather scientist who travels around looking for **tornadoes** and big thunderstorms to study	18
storm surge	a giant wave from the ocean that is pushed along by a **hurricane** A storm surge may cause flooding.	29
tornado	a spinning tower of very fast wind that moves along the ground Tornadoes often come out of thunderclouds.	4
tornado outbreak	ten or more **tornadoes** that happen in the same area over a few days	54
tornado swarm	a group of **tornadoes** that come from the same storm	53
tornado zone	an area where many **tornadoes** hit land	49
tropical cyclone	a giant storm with spinning winds **Hurricanes** and **typhoons** are both kinds of tropical cyclones. *Tropical cyclone* is also the name that is used for this kind of storm in Australia, India, and Bangladesh.	23

Word	Definition	Page
typhoon	a giant storm with spinning winds *Typhoon* is the name for **tropical cyclones** that are born over the Pacific Ocean.	24
vertical	up and down	44
waterspout	a kind of **tornado** that travels over water, not over land	42

About the Author

Alan Venable grew up in Pittsburgh, Pennsylvania. After college, he was a teacher in Africa and traveled in other parts of the world. He has written many books for Start-to-Finish, as well as plays, novels, and children's books. He has two children and lives in an old house in San Francisco, California.

About the Narrator

Denise Jordan-Walker worked as a
radio announcer in Chicago for over 15 years
before she started her own company in 1994.
Her company helps produce projects in
music, sports, film, theater, and publishing.
She has worked with many stars, including
the actors Bernie Mac, John Travolta, and
Angela Bassett, the basketball player Allen
Iverson, and musicians such as Chaka Kahn
and Billy Dee Williams.

A Note to the Teacher

Start-to-Finish Core Content books are designed to help students achieve success in reading to learn. From the provocative cover question to the carefully structured and considerate text, these books promote inquiry, active engagement, and understanding. Not only do students learn curriculum-relevant content, but they learn how to read with understanding. Here are some of the features that make these books such powerful aids in teaching and learning.

Structure That Supports Inquiry and Understanding

Core Content books are carefully structured to encourage students to ask questions, identify main ideas, and understand how ideas relate to one another. The structural features of the Gold Core Content books include the following:

- **"Getting Started"**: A concise introduction engages students in the book's topic and explicitly states what they will learn.
- **Clearly focused articles:** Each of the following articles focuses on a single topic at a length that makes for a comfortable session of reading.
- **"Questions This Article Will Answer"**: Provocative questions following the article title reflect the article's main ideas. Each question corresponds to a heading within the article.
- **Article introduction:** An engaging opening leads to a clear statement of the article topic.
- **Carefully worded headings:** The headings within each article are carefully worded to signal the main idea of the section and reflect the opening questions.
- **Clear topic statements:** Within each article section, the main idea is explicitly stated so that students can distinguish it from supporting details.
- **"Summary"**: A brief Summary in each article recaptures the main ideas signaled by the opening questions, text headings, and topic statements.

Text That Is Written for Success™

Every page of a Core Content book is the product of a skilled team of educators, writers, and editors who understand your students' needs. The text features of these books include the following:

- **Mature treatment of grade level curriculum:** Core Content is age and grade-appropriate for the older student who is actively acquiring reading skills. The books also contain information that may be new to any student in the class, empowering Core Content readers to contribute interesting information to class discussions.
- **Idioms and vocabulary:** The text limits the density of new vocabulary and carefully introduces new words, new meanings of familiar words, and idioms. New subject-specific terms are bold-faced and included in the Glossary.
- **Background knowledge:** The text assumes little prior knowledge and anchors the reader using familiar examples and analogies.
- **Sentence structure:** The text uses simple sentence structures whenever possible, but where complex sentences are needed to clarify links between ideas, the structures used are those which research has shown to enhance comprehension.

For More Information

To find out more about Start-to-Finish Core Content, visit www.donjohnston.com for full product information, standards and research base.